When the Owl Calls Your Name

ALAN SYLIBOY

NIMBUS
PUBLISHING
NIMBUS.CA

Nimbus Publishing Limited
3660 Strawberry Hill St, Halifax, NS, B3K 5A9
(902) 455-4286 nimbus.ca

Printed and bound in Canada.
Nimbus Publishing is based in Kjipuktuk, Mi'km'aki, the traditional territory of the Mi'kmaq People.

Editors: Lindsay Gloade-Raining Bird & Whitney Moran | Design: Heather Bryan | NB1720

Library and Archives Canada Cataloguing in Publication

Title: When the owl calls your name / Alan Syliboy.
Names: Syliboy, Alan, author.
Identifiers: Canadiana (print) 20230438393 | Canadiana (ebook) 20230438849
ISBN 9781774712467 (hardcover) | ISBN 9781774712474 (EPUB)
Subjects: LCSH: Songs, English—Canada—Texts. | CSH: Mi'kmaq—Social life and customs—Juvenile poetry. | LCGFT: Poetry. | LCGFT: Picture books.
Classification: LCC PS8637.Y39 W44 2023 | DDC jC811/.6—dc23

Nimbus Publishing acknowledges the financial support for its publishing activities from the Government of Canada, the Canada Council for the Arts, and from the Province of Nova Scotia. We are pleased to work in partnership with the Province of Nova Scotia to develop and promote our creative industries for the benefit of all Nova Scotians.

Dedicated to the memory of
Robert Denton
the original animator for "The Owl Song."
(1961–2022)

They say when the owl calls your name,

that the Creator is calling you home.

When the owl has your name,

he will come looking for you
wherever you are.

And when the owl comes to you,
he sits and waits until your
final breath.

Then your journey begins.

And you follow the owl high into
the sky, back to the Milky Way.

And you find the signpost
that brought you here.

And now will guide you
back to the Creator.

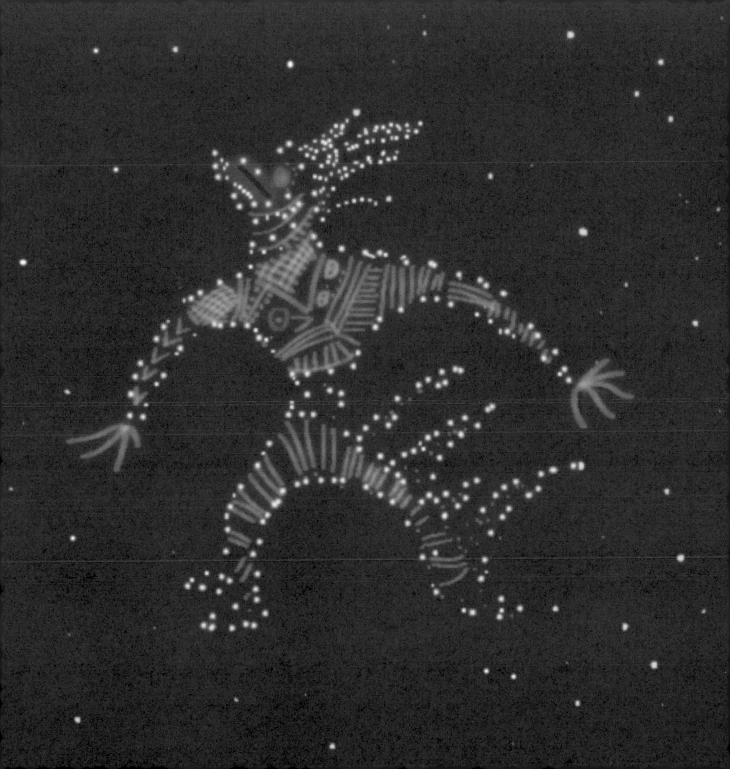

Your spirit is welcomed
by the ancient ones.

And you sit with them
by the council fire.

There's a place here
waiting for you.

There's a story the Mi'kmaq tell
about a child that passed away.

And they buried this child
beside a well-worn path.

And the reason for that
is that the spirit of this child
will be nourished by the women
walking on this path.

The owl flies on
silent wings,

so you may not know this owl
is coming for you.

So you must live your life in such a way

That you will be ready for the owl
when he calls your name.

A Note from Alan Syliboy

When someone from our community dies, Mi'kmaq people give thanks for the life of the deceased and help contribute to the crossing-over process. In Mi'kmaw culture, a person in the process of passing over destroys or disables their daily-use implements, like bowls and arrows, so they can never be used again. Then at the funeral ceremony, the community replaces these implements by offering gifts such as knives, bowls, and hunting bows and arrows. The person who is crossing over is also given goods and provisions for the journey to the Spirit World, and these items are buried with them. Everyone in the community plays a role in the crossing-over ceremony.

One traditional burial option is for a person to be buried sitting upright, facing east, with a birchbark shroud with red ochre placed over them. Red ochre is used so that they will be recognized by the Creator. Because the Mi'kmaq are the People of the Dawn and the Keepers of the Eastern Door, this type of burial holds spiritual meaning for us.

I once read a story about a priest who had a terminal illness. He was sent to an Indigenous village to learn about death. Part of his teachings were of the owl legend. This West Coast legend says that the Creator sends an owl to meet a person who is near death to deliver the message to each of us, when it is our turn, that "it is time to come home." The owl leads the spirit across the Milky Way back to the Creator, thereby completing the circle of life. I adapted those teachings to share this legend in "The Owl Song," which I often perform with my band, Alan Syliboy & the Thundermakers.

Death and crossing over are a part of life and we should be ready when our time comes.

Artist Alan Syliboy studied privately with Shirley Bear and attended the Nova Scotia College of Art and Design, where twenty-five years later, he was invited to sit on the Board of Governors. Alan looks to the indigenous Mi'kmaw petroglyph tradition for inspiration and develops his own artistic vocabulary out of those forms. He lives in Truro, Nova Scotia.

Other Books by Alan Syliboy

978-1-77108-889-3
7 x 7, Boardbook, Ages 0–3

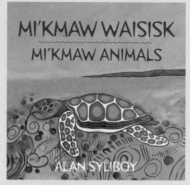

978-1-77108-641-7
7 x 7, Boardbook, Ages 0–3

978-1-77108-619-6
10 x 9, 32 pages, children's
picture book

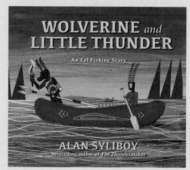

978-1-77471-090-6
10 x 9, 40 pages, children's
picture book

978-1-77108-649-3
Humpback Whale Journal
5.5 x 8, 192 pages, padded
cover w. ribbon marker